AROUND
WESTON -SUPER- MARE
IN OLD PHOTOGRAPHS

WESLEYAN CHAPEL. West Street, Banwell, c. 1905. Pictured here from left to right are: Mrs Cuff, Mrs Stockbridge, Mrs Neads, Miss Merrick and Miss Hemmins.

AROUND
WESTON -super- MARE
IN OLD PHOTOGRAPHS

COLLECTED BY
SHARON POOLE

ALAN SUTTON

Alan Sutton Publishing
Phoenix Mill · Far Thrupp · Stroud · Gloucestershire

First published 1989

Reprinted 1993

British Library Cataloguing in Publication Data

Around Weston-super-Mare in old photographs.
1. Avon. Weston-super-Mare, history
I. Poole, Sharon
942.3'96

ISBN 0-86299-586-8

Typesetting and origination by
Alan Sutton Publishing
Printed in Great Britain by
The Bath Press, Avon.

CONTENTS

THE ALMSHOUSES, WORLE. Mrs Bennett is seen here outside her home in The Scaurs. Note the communal water pump on the left.

TREE FELLING, C. 1912. Photographed in the heart of a felled tree at Pillhay Farm, Hewish, are members of the Cox family of Wick St Lawrence. Back row, left to right: Jack, George, Frank and James. Front row: Francis Cox and Colston Palmer.

INTRODUCTION

The area illustrated by the photographs in this book is the circle of villages and hamlets surrounding the popular seaside resort of Weston-super-Mare. This is a compact region naturally bounded by the River Axe and Mendip Hills to the south, and the River Yeo and the sea to the north and west respectively. Villages here hug the slopes of the limestone hills or are on islands of higher ground safe from the danger of flooding on the low marshy moor.

When I first started to compile the companion volume to this book (*Weston-super-Mare in Old Photographs*), I had intended to include photographs of Uphill and Worle as, although they have managed to retain their individual village identities to a degree, it is easy to think of them under the mantle of Weston-super-Mare. It soon became apparent that a small section in that book could in no way do justice to the wealth of material available, and so this book was conceived as a natural sequel. The scope of its subject matter has, however, been enlarged to cover all the adjacent villages from Kewstoke and its hamlet Milton, north to Wick St Lawrence, through Worle and travelling east to Locking, Banwell and Hutton to Uphill, concluding at Bleadon and Brean Down.

There is not the space here to give a detailed history of each village in what is one of the most fascinating parts of old Somerset. Nevertheless, a few background notes may be of interest and allow the photographs to tell their own story more eloquently.

In prehistoric times much of the area was very wet and prone to frequent flooding. Gradually, over the centuries, the sea-level fell and the land was drained.

This has left rich fertile deposits on the underlying peat and clay beds. People gradually moved into the region and settled on the dry higher ground. The earliest settlers we know of lived here during the Paleolithic age in caves found in Uphill Quarry. Later, Neolithic people farmed on Bleadon and Worle Hills, and, as time passed, settlements grew. During the Iron Age, it is likely that many villages and farms were built on the hills and lower slopes around the area. One of the surviving sites of this period is Worlebury Hillfort on Worle Hill, overlooking Weston-super-Mare and Kewstoke. In AD 43 the Romans invaded Britain and shortly afterwards they too established themselves here. There is a great variety of archaeological sites of this period in the area, with villas discovered at Banwell and Locking and a temple on Brean Down. The rivers Yeo, Banwell and Axe were navigable then and there may have been a small port at Uphill.

Life carried on in the region in the centuries after the Romans left Britain. New settlers arrived and the area came under Saxon rule. Christianity was spreading and from this time we have the first evidence for stave churches, with a piece of interlace sculpture found at Banwell.

The Domesday Book gives us some of the first tangible records of our district. The land was providing the greatest source of wealth as the rich grassy slopes of the uplands supported sheep. Wool was a very valuable crop in medieval times and many of the magnificent local churches were built with its profits. More traces of medieval occupation have been found in the villages than in Weston and it is clear that at this time places, such as Banwell, held a far greater importance than the insignificant fishing and farming village of Weston-super-Mare. By the mid-twelfth century most of the local churches had been built and their villages grew up around them. In the early thirteenth century Woodspring Priory was founded near Kewstoke and there were early medieval fortified towers or castles on the ring earthworks at Castle Batch near Worle and at Locking.

The fertile soil has always provided ideal conditions for agriculture and that forms the basic economy of the area. Once sea defences were erected to prevent constant inundation, the fields were drained by digging a system of ditches or rhynes. Cattle, both dairy and beef, were then grazed in the lush meadows. Fruit and vegetables grew in abundance and market gardens covered large parts of Milton, Kewstoke and Worle during the last century and the beginning of this. The hamlet of Norton between Kewstoke and Worle was particularly famed for its wheat and potato crops. Apple and pear orchards provided for cider and perry; the rhynes were fished for eels, a local delicacy. So, while in the nineteenth century Weston benefited from the 'discovery' of the seaside and realised its potential as a resort town, the local villages gained new markets for their produce and employment for their skills. Milton, for instance, became famed (or notorious) as the centre for washerwomen and laundresses and it was said that 'the intimate garments of half of Weston could be seen fluttering in the breeze.'

The villages also enjoyed some 'spin-off' tourism from Weston's boom. Most of the tourist guides to the town, in the nineteenth century, included detailed tours by foot, horseback, carriage or occasionally donkey. These covered a radius of several miles with notes on places of interest on the way. Some of the descriptions seem hard to reconcile with the sights of today and the quaint phrases make delightful reading now. In 1855, J. Whereat wrote, in his *New Handbook to Weston-super-*

Mare, that 'Irregular and scattered houses and cottages on the western declivity of the hill mark the little village of Bleadon'. Other places are described just as lyrically – 'A few scattered farm-houses and cottages constitute the village of Kewstoke, romantically situated at the foot of the lofty hill of Worle.' From the top of the newly cut road called Monks Hill he wrote of '. . . the moor beneath us, fields, yellow with golden grain, or bright with flowering clover, cultivated slopes, and grassy meadows, – while many old farmhouses, with dark russet thatch, scarcely perceptible amongst the embrowned foliage, ornament the landscape at different points.'

A few years later, in 1870, T. Beedle wrote a description of a walk from Weston to Worle '. . . After passing the turnpike gate, we cannot but notice the trim farmhouses on the roadside; whilst at the rear, on the slope of Worle Hill, are many private residences, which, on a fine day, present a very pretty effect, surrounded as they are with pasture lands.' He then went on to describe Banwell as '. . . a pretty village which derives its name from a spring or well, which forms a pond in the centre of the parish, and works a corn mill; the water also being used for brewing purposes.' After a sojourn at the Bell or Ship Inn, it was suggested that the traveller should then visit the famous Bone Caves discovered by William Beard in 1824. These were limestone caverns into which the bones of ice-age animals had been naturally washed and had collected in vast numbers. The way back was via Locking where '. . . the varied scenery, the snug-looking homesteads, and the fine large trees with their huge branches and foliage, offering a delightful shade to the wayfarer during the heat of the day, cannot fail to attract the attention of the tourist.'

A few industries were carried on in the region besides farming. These were mostly connected with the natural resources of the district. They included brick and tile manufacture using the local clay, and mineral mining. Calamine, a zinc ore used in the production of brass, was first discovered in England on Worle Hill in 1566, and lead and ochre were also extracted in the area. Worle Hill was also quarried for limestone, both for building stone and lime. Rutter, in his *Delineations of the County of Somerset*, written in 1829, speaks of Worle as '. . . sheltered from the sea wind, by its remarkable hill, crowned with a windmill; and rich in mines of lapis calaminaris and other ores. . . The Parish of Worle contains 130 houses, 140 families and 673 inhabitants.' A more clandestine occupation would have been smuggling. Many tales have been told of fishermen, or other locals, from Uphill to Wick St Lawrence, hastily hiding illicit barrels of liquor from the revenue men.

As Weston slowly grew, many hamlets and villages were engulfed by its spread. The ancient manor of Ashcombe and the settlement of Milton were among the first to be swallowed up, although Milton still had a separate listing in the town's directories as late as 1922. Development has physically connected Worle to Weston and now, as Worle itself grows so rapidly, one wonders how long it will be before Wick St Lawrence becomes another victim. Building at Kewstoke has swallowed up the tiny hamlets of Hatley and Norton; and Ebdon and Icelton are no more. The new proposals for housing to be built at Locking Castle will effectively turn that village into yet another suburb of Weston.

By contrast, some of the villages seem little changed since the early days of this century. For the present, Wick St Lawrence stands off the beaten track, with its fine thirteenth-century church tower rising above the surrounding fields and orchards.

Banwell too, is still a village of great charm with its winding lanes and old cottages. However, it still awaits a long promised bypass and meanwhile endures a heavy toll exacted by lorries and coaches thundering daily through its main street. Hutton meanders along the road repeatedly winning 'Best Kept Village' and 'Britain in Bloom' awards.

The sequence of pictures in this book take one on a roughly circular tour, with Weston at the centre and perhaps the odd diversion thrown in. It starts from the Toll-Road to Kewstoke and ends up at Brean Down and Bleadon. I hope you enjoy my selection, which was not easy to put together, but was great fun. Inevitably some photographs had to be left out, but I hope that what you see here conveys a little of the history and life of each place. Although the majority of the pictures come from the collections at Woodspring Museum, many also come from private individuals who have been most generous in lending their photographs for your pleasure. It has been a fascinating experience to stand in these villages today armed with the views of yesterday and to compare them. I hope that you too will visit these places and see them with new insight.

Sharon Poole 1989

SECTION ONE

Kewstoke and Sand Bay

THE WATERCRESS SELLER on the Toll Road from Weston-super-Mare to Kewstoke, c. 1900.

THE TOLL GATE, Kewstoke Road, Weston-super-Mare, c. 1915. In 1848 this road was made as a private drive through the game reserve, by John Hugh Smyth Pigott, the local lord of the manor. There was a lodge at each end for the gatekeepers. Pedestrians have never been charged a toll as the road follows the line of Black Rock Path, an old right-of-way.

THE TOLL GATE c. 1930. The Cliffs Cafe (now the Cosa Nostra Restaurant) has now been built on the seaward side of the road. Just disappearing round the corner can be seen one of Burnell & Company's busses, *en route* to Sand Bay. The Lodge on the right was demolished in 1967.

KEWSTOKE LODGE C. 1904. This gatekeeper's cottage was at the Kewstoke village end of the Toll Road. Thomas Barry was the first toll-collector to live here with his wife Harriet, in 1848.

CULLING'S CAFE, Kewstoke, C. 1947. This was situated at the Kewstoke end of the Toll Road. The castellated building on the right was the Castle Restaurant, built next to the old Lodge, pictured above, and in a similar style.

KEWSTOKE VILLAGE c. 1880. The building to be glimpsed to the left, under the tree, was used as a poorhouse during the seventeenth and eighteenth centuries. It was converted into Kewstoke's first schoolroom in 1840. The sign on the right reads 'To the New Inn'.

KEWSTOKE FROM THE HILL, c. 1907.

ST PAUL'S CHURCH. Of Norman origin, the church is mainly thirteenth century with fourteenth- and fifteenth-century alterations and additions.

KEWSTOKE VILLAGE from Monks Hill, c. 1903. Note the row of bee hives in the cottage garden to the right in the foreground. Sand Bay can be seen on the horizon.

HOME FARM, AUGUST 1885. This farm was owned by the Smyth Pigotts and in the 1880s was leased to the Stabbins family. In around 1890 the owners built a new farmhouse (now the Owls Crest Hotel). In 1914 the whole Smyth Pigott estate was put up for sale and Home Farm was bought by William Weaver for £830. Various items of farm equipment can be seen in this picture – barrels for cider, a water pump, a light cart (with its shafts up) and a plough, the handle of which is to the left of the children. The man is carrying a flail, used for threshing grain.

HOME FARM in the 1880s. This is the same farmyard as that in the picture on the left. Here it is looking a little tidier. The farmhouse was built in the seventeenth century.

KEWSTOKE CHAPEL, C. 1889. This chapel was built in around 1880 for the non-conformist members of the community. It is seen here on its original site just above Victory Cottages and next to Orchard Cottage on land belonging to Ardnave Farm. In 1902 they moved to a new hall opposite the top of Crookes Lane. The chapel was linked to the Brethren movement and preachers came from Waterloo Hall in Weston-super-Mare.

THE NEW COUNCIL SCHOOL. This opened on 1 September 1909. It was built because the existing school at Milton Hill had become overcrowded.

CHILDREN AT KEWSTOKE SCHOOL, January 1925.

THE NEW INN, Crookes Lane, C. 1947. This inn was built on the site of a much earlier tavern.

Kewstoke Church & Village

KEWSTOKE CHURCH and village, C. 1910. Victory Cottages can be seen on the right. These were built in 1759, the date of General Wolfe's victory at the Battle of Quebec in Canada. The top and handle of the village pump can just be glimpsed beside the woman on the right.

KEWSTOKE VILLAGE, C. 1911. The Post Office is on the left of this photograph. A large private carriage is in the centre of the road, with part of Home Farm on the right.

KEWSTOKE POST OFFICE, C. 1910. This was at Canterbury Cottage and was run at this time by Mr Dowden, seen here leaning against the sign.

KEWSTOKE VILLAGE from Monks Hill, c. 1914. The tiny group of fishermen's cottages on the horizon, to the left of the taller house, are said to have been built in 1663. In the early 1960s they were greatly extended and altered to make the Commodore Hotel.

KEWSTOKE AND SAND BAY from Worle Hill. The compact form of the old village can clearly be seen here.

SAND BAY, c. 1920. The area, once only farms and fields, is here beginning to be built on. The road along the beach peters out to a footpath on the left, the only road access being along Crookes Lane at this date.

THE NEW BUNGALOWS at Beach Road, Sand Bay. These were built in the 1920s and 1930s.

ONE OF THE HOLIDAY CHALETS in Sand Bay, c. 1920. The fishermen's cottages in the left background were later converted into the Commodore Hotel.

CLYNTONVILLE GUEST HOUSE. The tennis court and gardens are pictured here c. 1931. Clyntonville was on the southern corner of Crookes Lane and Beach Road.

THE KEWSTOKE CONVALESCENT HOME FOR WOMEN. This was opened on 1 July 1933. It was built, at a cost of £60,000, to house convalescent members of the Birmingham Hospital Saturday Fund. It was opened by Sir Charles Hyde, Bt., a Birmingham newspaper owner and philanthropist.

A SIDE VIEW of the new Convalescent Home, soon after its building and before occupation. It had 179 rooms with beds for 100 patients.

THE LOUNGE of the Convalescent Home. This was very luxurious for its day and boasted a polished wooden floor and baby grand piano.

THE LIBRARY at the Convalescent Home. Patients stayed for two weeks at a time.

WOODSPRING PRIORY, c. 1900. The Priory began life as a chapel dedicated to St Thomas à Becket attached to the manor of Woodspring. In the thirteenth century William de Courtney, lord of the manor, converted the chapel into an Augustinian Priory and donated the land to the religious order.

THE TITHE BARN at Woodspring Priory, c. 1900. Much of the priory was rebuilt in the fifteenth century and most of the remains are of this date. The priory was dissolved in 1536 and was used for a time as a hospital. It was rehallowed in December 1970.

THE FARMHOUSE AND WEST FRONT at Woodspring Priory. The farmhouse was built in 1701 by the Smyth Pigott family, then lords of the manor. The priory is now owned by the Landmark Trust and is open to the public.

COLLUM FARM, C. 1911. This farm is on the road from Kewstoke and Worle to Woodspring Priory.

KEWSTOKE FROM MONKS STEPS. Monks Hill is in the foreground. The old village pond can just be seen, glistening in the sun, to the left of Crookes Lane.

MONKS HILL C. 1915. This road from Kewstoke Village up Worle Hill to Worlebury, was cut in 1853, under the powers of the Kewstoke Enclosure Act. Part of Monks Steps was destroyed in the process. It is the steepest hill in the area with a gradient of 1 in 4.

MONKS HILL SWALLET. This cave was discovered in 1927 by the Reverend Doorbar, Vicar of Kewstoke, pictured here with his helpers. Close to Monks Steps, it was first broken into in 1853 during the building of Monks Hill, but it was filled up again. It was hoped it would lead to a much larger cavern with remains of prehistoric animals, but they only found a small stalactite cavern.

ST PAUL'S CHURCH, c. 1910. The path of Monks Steps can clearly be seen up the hillside.

MONKS STEPS, C. 1907. This ancient pathway, roughly built from unhewn rocks, was probably built as the old church-way from the settlement of Milton on the other side of the hill, to their parish church at Kewstoke.

SECTION TWO

Milton

FORE STREET, Milton, c. 1916. Now called Baytree Road, the houses on the right, including Mr Chorley's shop, were demolished in 1961 for road improvements. Note the Shell petrol pump (with the white globe on top).

UPPER BRISTOL ROAD, 1920. This photograph has been taken from just past Ashbury Drive, with no. 41 Bristol Road on the left. The houses in the distance are in the Crescent.

UPPER BRISTOL ROAD, c. 1916. This view has actually changed very little. Mr Curry's shop is now a fish & chip take-away.

THE GROVE, GROVE ROAD, c. 1910. Owned and run by Miss Gandy and Fräulein Klausmann, the Milton Gardening School taught techniques of horticulture. It had its own fruit garden, orchard and greenhouses. The school also ran a shop in Regent Street, Weston, to sell the produce. It closed just before the First World War.

ST JUDE'S CHURCH AND TERRACE, c. 1920. This pretty church was built in 1886. Before that date Milton church-goers had to use their parish church in Kewstoke. Since it closed in the late 1970s, St Jude's has become the Greek Orthodox church for Weston-super-Mare.

THE WINDSOR CASTLE HOTEL C. 1907. The proprietor of the hotel has just changed from Fred Goodyear to W. Hislop. The man on the horse on the right is John Edwards of Kewstoke.

THE WINDSOR CASTLE again, pictured in the late 1920s. The Hotel started life as the Masons Arms, probably linked to the large number of stone quarries in the area. The castellated frontage is a later addition.

GENERAL VIEW OF MILTON from Worle Hill, c. 1920. Some of the many market gardens can be seen here. The white building to the left is the Windsor Castle Hotel. St Jude's Church is at the bottom of the road in the foreground.

GENERAL VIEW OF MILTON from Spring Hill.

THE LIMESTONE QUARRIES C. 1908. Run by Henry Butt & Co., these were a major source of male employment at Milton.

LIME KILNS, Butt's Quarry.

MILTON RISE C. 1926. These council houses were built in 1922. A Weston-super-Mare Co-op van can just be seen on the left.

UNDERWOOD AVENUE C. 1928. This was a private development of bungalows.

STAPLES' DAIRIES no. 217, Milton Road, pictured here in July 1948.

ONE OF THE MILK FLOATS belonging to Staples' Dairies of Milton and Manor House Farm, Worle.

MILTON METHODIST CHURCH. Built to replace an old Mission Room, at a cost of £3,300, this church was opened on 9 October 1930. The site was given by Henry Butt, Weston's first Mayor, in exchange for the old building, which then became a public hall.

LAYING A COMMEMORATIVE STONE at Milton Methodist Church on 16 December 1950. In June 1942 the old church (pictured above) was destroyed by a German bomb. Here, Mrs Staples of Staples' Dairies, is laying one of the commemorative stones in the new church, which opened on 28 September 1951.

HOME FARM C. 1910. The Dyer family pose outside their home, which they leased from the Smyth Pigott estate. The farmhouse still exists, at the bottom of Baytree Road, on the corner of Drysdale Close.

WESTON, CLEVEDON & PORTISHEAD LIGHT RAILWAY ENGINE *Clevedon*, at Milton Crossing, 1900. On the footplate are driver, Jack Jones and fireman, W. Preston. The engine was built by Sharp Steward & Co., Manchester and was bought second-hand by the WCPLR from the Furness Railway in 1898.

Wick St Lawrence

THE VILLAGE CROSS AND CHURCH of St Lawrence, Wick St Lawrence, c. 1906.

THE WRECK OF THE *HESPERUS*, 1934. On 5 April that year, WCPLR locomotive *Hesperus* was heading for the Wick St Lawrence jetty with loaded goods wagons, when the recently renovated wooden bridge over the East Town Rhyne collapsed under the weight. It took three days to slowly jack up the engine and salvage her.

WICK ST LAWRENCE HALT on the Weston, Clevedon & Portishead Light Railway. This provided the only direct link between these three towns and was the main means of transporting the farm produce and milk until the 1930s.

CEDARS FARM, 1921. Pictured from a sale catalogue, this dairy farm opposite the church was sold to Mrs Edwards for £4,200.

THE OSMOND FAMILY outside Appleton Farm, c. 1900. Back row, left to right: John, Beatrice, William, Percy, Bertram. Middle row: Harold, Florence, Emily, Albert, Ethel. Front row: Reginald, Millicent.

MARY BALLAM at Wick St Lawrence village pump. This was situated outside the school.

WICK ST LAWRENCE SCHOOL, C. 1906.

WILFRED BALLAM son of Mary (pictured left), outside his home in School Lane, in 1915.

WICK ST LAWRENCE SCHOOL, 1924. Back row, left to right: Dan Stabbins, Bill Hooper, Fred Wride, Sid Stabbins, Jack Bishop. Middle row: Sam Rattle, Jack Osmond, Bill Parsons, Sarah Bonell (head mistress), Dorothy Parsons, Amy Murray (school mistress), Cecil Parsons, Henry Parsons, Jim Stabbins. Front row: Sid Rattle, ? Locke, Norah Beecham, Frances Chaplin, Ron Edwards, Margaret Payne, Betty Davis, Katherine Kingsbury, -?-, Rose Kimmins.

WICK ST LAWRENCE SUNDAY SCHOOL on an outing to Congresbury Church and vicarage, c. 1890.

THE BELLS from Wick St Lawrence Church. Two of the bells were made in 1736 and 1761 by the famous Bilbie family of bell-founders and clockmakers, at Chew Stoke. The bells were photographed here in a local cider orchard by Hardwick & Co. of Weston-super-Mare, before being rehung by the firm of Llewellins and James in 1910.

SAM DAVIS, farmer at Wick St Lawrence, at the Christmas Fatstock Market in Weston-super-Mare. The other people pictured are, from the left: Reg Clarke, Lewis Edwards, -?-, John Ballam.

MYRTLE COTTAGE, Icelton, 1921. At this time it was the residence of the Revd E.J. Lutley.

Worle

MANCHESTER SQUARE, c. 1900. This was named after Manchester House, later known as Gunnings Stores, and situated on the corner here. The lean-to building to the left of the man was Mr Broadbear's butcher's shop. Mendip View (now Bell House), facing, is reputed to be the oldest house in the village. This late medieval home has the remains of a cruck-frame construction.

LAWRENCE ROAD. Of all the cottages shown in this view only Rock Cottage (in the centre) and Maywood (on the right) remain.

THE OLD FORGE, Kewstoke Road. This was demolished in 1973 for road improvements. Springwell Cottage is on the right.

CHURCH ROAD EAST. This view has hardly changed, at a superficial glance. The thatched roof on the cottages has gone however. The three-storey building used to be the Valiant Soldier Inn. Dated 1670, Judge Jeffries is reputed to have stayed there during part of the Bloody Assizes. Note the old bakery and shop to the right. This burnt down and was converted into two cottages in 1931. The white house at the end of the road is Maywood, now derelict and the subject of a planning controversy.

ST MARTIN'S CHURCH, C. 1905. This twelfth-century church was largely restored in 1870.

HILL ROAD, C. 1901. The school can just be seen on the left.

WORLE SCHOOL, Hill Road, c. 1906. This building included part of an old monastic barn, restored for use in 1866. The school was further enlarged in 1911, to cater for 258 children.

CHILDREN AT WORLE SCHOOL, c. 1909. They have obviously been dressed in their best clothes for this picture. Some of the girls even have flowers fastened to their pinafores.

FERN LEA, Lawrence Road.

LAWRENCE ROAD, Worle, c. 1906. The tall building in the centre is the Ebenezer Chapel.

THE EBENEZER CHAPEL, Lawrence Road.

VIEW FROM LAWRENCE ROAD, c. 1910. Myrtle Cottage is in the centre, with the village constable's home behind it. Worle Church can just be seen on the left.

LOWER STREET, with The Parade in the centre. The Lamb Inn is in the distance with the Capital & Counties Bank on the right.

THE LAMB INN, Lower Street.

LOWER STREET, with the malthouse and boot factory. The New Inn (now The Woodspring) is on the left, advertising a large room for picnics, parties etc. Gas pipes are being laid in Station Road. The cart driver is John Baker.

ANOTHER VIEW OF LOWER STREET, C. 1910. Note the road sweeper and one of the parish pumps on the right.

BOLTONS TERRACE, Coronation Road. A view looking south, c. 1913. This road was named after the coronation of Edward VII in 1902. The headlines on the newspaper placards read 'Russia's Four Dreadnoughts' and 'Premier heckled by Suffragettes.' The two ladies on the right are from Lyndhurst School, run by Miss Corfe and situated on the corner of Coronation Road.

CORONATION ROAD, looking north, c. 1905.

W.G. MOORE'S BUTCHER'S SHOP. Later Dennis', they had their own slaughterhouse which was demolished in 1977 for the Maltings development.

MEAT DISPLAY, High Street, 1936. Some of the labels on the tinned goods read 'Young Carrots 9d.' (4½p) and 'Garden peas 1s.4½d.' (7p).

MR G.R. PARKER'S BAKERY and confectioners shop, Worle High Street.

MRS PARKER'S CAKE STALL at a bazaar to raise money to build Worle Village Club.

THE WORLE GENERAL SUPPLY STORES, c. 1895. Later known as Gunnings Stores, this shop, situated in Manchester Square at the top of The Scaurs, is one of the oldest shops in the area. Pictured standing at the door is Annie Jervis Tucker, later Mrs Spinner. J.W. Spinner took over the business from James Irish in 1895. The complex included a store, granary, bakery, slaughterhouse and butcher's shop. It closed in 1985 and at present is being converted into residential units.

BRISTOL ROAD AND VICARAGE, C. 1918. The Capital & Counties Bank is on the left. Note the unsurfaced road.

ONE OF THE MANY PRETTY STONE COTTAGES that used to line the High Street. This one was opposite the entrance to what is now The Maltings.

LOWER STREET, c. 1910. The chimney of the laundry is just visible, with the New Inn (now the Woodspring) in the far distance.

LOWER STREET decorated for the coronation of Edward VII in 1902. The arch advertised a sheep-shearing competition.

THE SCAURS, C. 1919. Walter Hack is on the right, with Mr A. Lee, wearing a bowler hat, on the left. Mr Lee owned a lot of property in Worle, including the almshouses in the centre right of this picture. Mr Vincent is standing outside his shop.

THE SQUARE, C. 1920. A group of errand boys are standing by the wall with Charlie Knight, the water boy (see page 68), who is carrying two buckets from a yoke on his shoulders.

THE OLD KING'S HEAD, The Scaurs, Worle, 1909. A. Wyatt is the licensee. The poster beside the door is a timetable for the Weston, Clevedon & Portishead Light Railway, which had a station at Worle. The man beside the cart appears to be holding a bundle of gin traps.

THE HIGH STREET. Local lads home on Christmas leave during the First World War. Pictured outside Horril's tackshop, the group includes Reg Bray and Edward Burden. Note the bunches of mistletoe and holly on their caps and cycle handlebars.

THE NEWTONS. Situated between Worle and Kewstoke, this medieval manor house was substantially rebuilt in 1710 by John Selwood. The estate is some 700 years old. Today, the fine avenue of elms has gone and the house is surrounded by modern housing estates.

SPRING HILL C. 1937.

PREANES GREEN. Note the sewer pipes, on the left, ready to be laid. Preanes Green Lodge is in the centre on this view.

J. THYER'S DAIRY AND SHOP, Kewstoke Road, Mr Thyer and Mr Chapman are seen here.

CHARLIE KNIGHT, the water boy. Prior to 1914, Worle residents relied entirely on local wells for drinking water. This had to be fetched from various pumps around the village. The Methodist minister, Reverend Chapman, is on the left.

BRISTOL ROAD (now the High Street), c. 1917. Martins Grove now runs off to the left. The gabled building in the centre is the Golden Lion Inn. The house on the right is no longer there.

ENTRANCE TO WESTON WOODS, Worlebury. Another of the gatekeeper's lodges to the Smyth Pigott game reserve (see page 13). Here it has been turned into a tea-room.

WORLE STATION. This was built in 1884 by the Great Western Railway, on the new loop line into Weston-super-Mare. It is pictured here after closure in around 1923.

WORLE SIGNAL BOX in 1896. Passing the box is the last train to run on Brunel's original broad-gauge line, before total conversion to standard gauge. Here the tracks have been laid for both gauges. Mr Bowden, the signalman, is seen leaning out of the window.

STATION ROAD. White House Farm is on the left, and Laurel Farm on the right. The boy with the barrow is probably going to fetch some coal from the gasworks.

THE GASWORKS, Station Road, c. 1901.

KEWSTOKE ROAD, then called Hill Road, c. 1908. The cottages on the left have been demolished and Esgar Rise now runs off on the left.

KEWSTOKE ROAD, c. 1910. This terrace of houses is still to be seen, much as it was built. The top of the Observatory can just be glimpsed on the hilltop to the right of the house in the foreground.

WORLE QUARRY, c. 1904. The house is Hillend.

LYNCH FARM QUARRY. Note the pigs and ducks wandering freely.

MANOR FARM, 1914. In a sale brochure at the time, the farm is described as having five bedrooms, three garret rooms, dining and drawing rooms, kitchen with fixed range and dresser, dairy, larder, scullery etc. It was turned into an inn and hotel in 1981.

COURT FARM, c. 1890. This farm was on the corner of Madam Lane and was the home of the Day family at this time.

THE OBSERVATORY, c. 1909. This old windmill was built in 1765, to replace an earlier mill which had burnt down. It had one pair of stones, two dressing and smut machines and supplied its own bakery in the village. It was offered for sale in 1889 and converted into an observatory.

MOOR LANE with Vale Windmill in the distance, c. 1910. Some little conical haystacks are in the field on the right of the road.

MR QUICK BESIDE VALE WINDMILL, Moor Lane. Vale Mill was built in around 1813. Mr Quick took over the mill from his father in around 1880 and worked it until around 1910. Although a windmill, Mr Quick briefly experimented with steam power in 1889. This was not a success, however, and the mill was converted back again to wind power. The sails were removed in 1922 and stored. The machinery remained intact until a serious fire gutted the building in 1962, after which the mill was converted into a home.

Locking and Banwell

PUPILS AT LOCKING SCHOOL, photographed by the church gate in 1910. Back row, left to right: Fred Millier, Jack Venn, Albert Clark, Jack Glimstead. Third row: Gladys Venn, Violet Raines, Ella House, Mabel Choules, Annie Rowley, Florence Clark (teacher). Second row: Edith Stone, Evelyn Clark, Lucy Millier, Daisy Raines, Olive Raines, John Raines. Front row: Frank Millier, Cecil Glimstead, Reg Cook.

LOCKING MANOR, c. 1890. Home of the Plumley family for generations, the lands were confiscated by the Crown in 1685 for the family's part in the Monmouth Rebellion. John Plumley joined the rebels. His two sons died at the Battle of Sedgemoor but John escaped to the village, only to be betrayed by his dog. He was hanged and it is said that his grieving widow threw herself and the dog down the manor's well. The ladies under the tree are Miss Gingingham (left) and Miss Johnson.

LOCKING MANOR, c. 1890. Miss Gingingham is seated in the carriage, with Miss Johnson (standing) and Ponsford, the groom, holding the horse.

THE STONE CIRCLE, Locking Manor, c. 1890. It is said that this circle was brought down from Mendip in the early nineteenth century by the then owner of Locking Manor, Reverend Stiverd Jenkins. However, modern day historians think this is unlikely and that it is a folly.

LOCKING RAF CAMP, C. 1947. This unofficial photograph was taken from the top of the water tower. The camp opened on 27 January 1939, with the formation of No. 5 School of Technical Training.

RECRUITS AT RAF LOCKING, summer 1947. Members of Hut 22, No. 1 Entry including Messrs: Plowman, Green, Hendrich, Higate, Harrow, Peet, Foreman, Jones, Magor, Govan, Morgan, Honeyman, Mills, Maynard, Jackson, Holt, Jeffrey and Newson.

LOCKING RAF CAMP. No. 2 Wing Hobbies Club building a model of the escort sloop HMS *Weston* in 1942. The real ship was 'adopted' by the town of Weston-super-Mare, which raised over £400,000 to 'buy' her during Warship Week. The builders of the model were Flt. Sgt. Smith, Sgt. S. Allwright. ACL Bateman and ACL Ryall. The hull was made from driftwood, while other materials used varied from curtain rings to part of a German Junkers 88 aircraft. The model has survived in the collections of Woodspring Museum.

WRECKED BIPLANE. This aircraft crashed near Banwell during the First World War.

MAKING CIDER, C. 1910. John Millard and Tom Street, with a rare beam cider press, at Church Farm, Locking.

ST AUGUSTINE'S CHURCH, c. 1906.

THE INTERIOR of St Augustine's Church, c. 1906.

WESTON-SUPER-MARE GAS COMPANY EMPLOYEES, 1933. Workmen laying a high pressure main extension to Banwell, photographed on the old road near Locking RAF Camp. Back row, left to right: Mr Kitley, Bert Gregory, Mr Sperrings, Bill Crossman, Eli Drewitt, Mr Williams, Alfie Clapp, Ernest Baker, Mr Cross. Second row: Paddy Clout, Harry Finch, Walt Harris, Eddie Hole, Evan Howells, William Miller, William Neathway, Ernest Williams, Bob Jarvis, Paddy O'Flynn, Harry Cole, Ernest Brooks, Bill Tucker. Third row: Mr Baker, Syd Collard, Bob Crocker, Mr Woolmington, Rhys Brittain, Mr Hillier, Percy Gould. Front row: Sam Collard, Alf Maynard, Tom Palmer, Jim Griffin, Mr Wiltshire, Bill Knight, Mr Lawrence, Alec Bateman.

BANWELL FROM THE HILL, c. 1895. In the centre is the fourteenth-century tower of St Andrew's Church. Banwell Abbey can be seen to the right of the church.

BANWELL CASTLE. This Victorian folly was built in 1845 by Mr Simpson, on the site of an old farmhouse.

AN EXCURSION WAGONETTE, THE ROSA-BELLA, at Banwell, c. 1905, on its way to Cheddar from Weston-super-Mare. It paused at Banwell for a photograph to be taken by Fred Amos of the Mendip Studio, Banwell.

CHARABANC TOUR, c. 1922. A motor excursion to Cheddar Caves from Weston-super-Mare, in a 'Pride of the West' vehicle. It was photographed by A. Hardwick of Banwell, beside the wall where the school is now. Note the maximum speed of the vehicle – 12mph!

THE SHIP INN. Excursion wagonettes pause while their passengers refresh themselves inside, c. 1907.

A MEET OF THE BANWELL HUNT, outside the Ship Inn, 1937.

BANWELL TRADERS – above are Mr Creighton, wheelwright and Mr Clark, shoemaker, pictured in 1935. Below is Mr Dunn's Supply Stores, c. 1910.

MR HOLLYMAN'S SADDLERY SHOP, West Street, Banwell, c. 1920. Note the old mounting block on the kerbside.

THE SQUARE, c. 1910. Until 1798, a market cross stood in the centre here.

WEST STREET, from the Square. The Bell Hotel is on the right, with a wagonette full of passengers outside.

EAST STREET, 1905. A view looking towards Sandford. The shop on the right was a butcher's, now demolished for road widening.

WEST STREET, c. 1926. Mr Clark's shoe shop is on the left, (no relation to the well-known shoe firm).

CASTLE HILL, c. 1905. Pictured at the castle entrance is one of the Sugg boys (standing left). Harry Stephens is standing beside his cart, with Mr D. Cuff. The other vehicle was just passing by.

MR FEAR of Banwell, with his donkey cart, c. 1900.

BANWELL SCHOOLCHILDREN, c. 1900. They are holding copies of books with such titles as *British History, Robinson Crusoe* and *Courage and Peril.*

BANWELL SCOUTS, c. 1925. Back row, left to right: Mr Pruen (scoutmaster), Arnold Raines, Jack Neads, Victor Appleby, Barry Pruen, 'Ginger' Harris, Bert Keates, Andrew Williams, Peter Fry, Mrs Pruen (scoutmistress), Harry Marshall. Middle Row: Jim Harris, Raymond Harris, -?-, Cecil Tozer, Ivor Shallish. Front row: Reginald Shallish, Jack Shallish, Jack Stock, 'Ginger' Nuttycombe.

BANWELL POND, C. 1902. This pond was fed by a spring, which is now piped and supplies Weston-super-Mare with some of its water today. In the nineteenth century this spring worked a grist mill and brewery. The island was added in 1810. The area of the pond is today a bowling green.

BANWELL, C. 1905. A wintry scene outside the mill and brewery.

PARK COTTAGE, East Street, c. 1870. Later called Woodlands, this thatched house was the home of the Emery family.

BANWELL WOODS, c. 1920. This cottage, at the top of the hill opposite the castle, was the last thatched cottage in the village.

KEECHING THE RIVER BANWELL, *c.* 1920. Keeching is a local term for cleaning out rhynes, ditches and rivers. Pictured third from the left is George Parsley. On the bank is John Hicks (centre) and M. Tozer (right).

HARVESTING AT WINTHILL FARM, *c.* 1914. Left to right: -?-, G. Counsell, Ivy Salter, Kathleen Counsell, Mr Salter. The name of the man on the binder is not known.

SHEEP-SHEARING IN THE ORCHARD behind the Smiths Arms, Knightcott. Left to right: Mr Davis, Mr Nuttycombe, Charlie Watts, Mr Davis.

THE SMITHS ARMS, Knightcott. This building was demolished in 1970 and the Whistling Duck pub built on the site.

WORKMEN REPAIRING BANWELL ABBEY, C. 1905. Amongst those pictured are Messrs: Bill Brown (seated centre with white apron) C. Hunt, Stock, Harris and Pople. In the back row are Messrs: Nuttycombe, Leaker, Merrick, Warburton, Lancaster and White.

CELEBRATIONS to mark the relief of Mafeking, 1900. This gathering marched right around the village to celebrate this victory of the Boer War. An effigy was carried, with a boar's head, to represent the Boers.

Above; CHURCH STREET (left) and HIGH STREET (right), at the foot of Hill Path.
Below; THE GATEWAY TO THE CAVES, once home of Bishop Law of Bath & Wells and the site of the discovery of caves filled with remains of early animals.

CHURCH STREET. The funeral procession of Mr R. Clark. Mr Clark was killed by a German bomb, which fell on Banwell in 1940, while he was on duty as a Special Constable.

SECTION SIX

Hutton and Oldmixon

CORNER COTTAGE, Hutton c. 1910. This picturesque home was on the corner of Moor Lane. The man standing in the lane is Bill Palmer, the wheelwright. The Old Inn is in the distance. Note the old mounting steps beside the signpost.

OLDMIXON FARM, C. 1924. This building was demolished in 1966 and the Walnut Tree Inn built on the site.

MR R. COUNSELL at Oldmixon Farm, C. 1924.

OLDMIXON VILLAGE PUMP, 1935.

HUTTON VILLAGE, C. 1914.

MRS CORNER and her daughter at the blacksmith's workshop, Hutton, in the 1930s.

HAYMAKING ON WINDMILL HILL, C. 1925. Mr Corner and family, of the Smithy, Hutton.

MISS HEMBRY of Middle Farm, Hutton, in the 1930s.

MAIN ROAD, Hutton. The post office is on the right.

THE POST OFFICE, C. 1906. This is on the main road through the village, looking towards Hutton Hill.

HUTTON YOUTH HOSTEL. This was at the end of Eastfield Road. It closed in the 1960s and is now a private residence called 'Woodspring Lodge'.

CHURCH LANE, Hutton, c. 1911.

HUTTON COURT, c. 1912. Parts of this building date back to the fifteenth century, when it was the manor house for the village. It is possibly the oldest domestic building in this part of the county. It is now a hotel and restaurant.

HUTTON COURT, c. 1910. The hall and tower were built in around 1480, when John Payne was lord of the manor.

HUTTON COURT, C. 1907. The Bisdee family have tea on the lawn. Thomas and Edith Bisdee are to the right, with their children and some cousins.

THE STABLES at Hutton Court, C. 1905.

KANGAROOS at Hutton Court, c. 1910. When Thomas Bisdee inherited Hutton Court from his uncle, Edward, he brought his family back from Tasmania where they had a large property. He also brought back these four kangaroos. They lived in the stable field for many years and were eventually passed on to zoos on Thomas' death.

HUTTON CHURCH AND COURT, c. 1914. St Mary's Church is mainly fifteenth-century with a fine Perpendicular period tower.

MOORLANDS, Hutton, c. 1904. This fine Georgian house was built in around 1830 as a gentleman's residence with its own coach house and stable.

HUTTON VILLAGE, C. 1911.

THE OLD FARM STORES, Hutton, photographed in the 1930s. Note the fine 1921 design telephone kiosk to the left.

Uphill

UPHILL OLD CHURCH, 1856. The roof was removed in 1864 due to its dilapidated and dangerous state. The building was later used as a mortuary chapel for many years. A woman, dressed in a crinoline, may just be seen by the porch.

THE SHIP INN, UPHILL, C. 1890. There has been a pub on this site for over 200 years, although this building dates from around 1830.

THE SHIP INN, Uphill. In this view the building has been decorated for the coronation of King George V in June 1911.

UPHILL WAY from the Old Church, with the Ship Inn in the centre.

THORNBURY ROAD, pictured shortly after building at the beginning of this century. The land was originally part of Uphill Brickworks, with claypits spreading over much of this area.

Uphill, Weston-super-Mare.

ONE OF THE OLD CLAYPITS at Uphill Brickworks, c. 1910.

THE LIMESTONE QUARRIES, Uphill, c. 1918. The farmland on the left belonged to Slimeridge Farm, seen here in the distance among the trees.

UPHILL WHARF from the hill, c. 1925. This wharf was used mainly for the export of stone and lime from the quarry, and bricks and tiles from the brickworks. In return, Welsh coal and slate were imported.

THIS PHOTOGRAPH is believed to show the old Schoolhouse and cottage, just to the south of Uphill Manor. Built in the late seventeenth century, the building was later run as a charity school for children of the poor.

UPHILL SCHOOL, c. 1907. A wintry scene in the playground. The school was built in 1872 by the Knyfton family of Uphill Manor. An extra classroom was added in 1889. It is now Uphill Primary School.

A GARDENING CLASS at Uphill School, c. 1906. The tower of St Nicholas Church can just be seen on the right.

A CALLISTHENICS CLASS exercise in the playground at Uphill School using indian clubs.

UPHILL WAY, c. 1890. This photograph was taken from the corner of Old Church Road, with the Dolphin Inn on the left. The Ship Inn is in the distance.

CENTRE FARM in the 1890s. Mr Counsell is seen here with his son. The farm was in Uphill Way to the right of the Ship Inn.

UPHILL WAY, C. 1918. Ynisher Terrace (right) was built in 1911.

UPHILL WAY, 1921. A view looking in the opposite direction to that above.

WORKMEN IN UPHILL, fencing, building and laying new sewer pipes in Old Church Road.

UPHILL JUNCTION SIGNAL BOX. Two broad-gauge trains can be seen here – one on the main line from Bristol and another on the loop line into Weston Station. Note the dual-gauge track, prior to complete conversion to standard gauge in 1896. These trains were photographed on 4 September 1891.

UPHILL MANOR. This was built in 1805 and a school for the gentry was established there by the Reverend Gegg. In 1825 it was bought by Thomas Knyfton who added the tower and castellations. It is still owned by his descendants.

UPHILL ROAD SOUTH, 27 June 1927. This postcard view was entitled 'Your Licence Please'.

UPHILL RECTORY, 1904. This was the second of Uphill's three rectories and stood where St Aubyns Avenue is now. The Rector, Reverend Burr, is seated in the doorway with his dog.

THE DONKEY FIELD, C. 1927. Some of Weston-super-Mare's beach donkeys were wintered in this field opposite Uphill Manor.

THE BELLS from the old church of St Nicholas. In 1914 the bells were retuned and rehung at a cost of £338 10s. At this time a sixth bell was added (foreground of picture), as a gift from Charles E. Whitting of Uphill Grange. Four of the five original bells were cast by William Bilbie, one of the famous Chew Stoke family of bell-founders and clock makers.

TOTTERDOWN, c. 1910. Above and below left are the playing fields and gardens at the School, Totterdown Hall. Below right is a view of Totterdown Avenue, c. 1910.

POSTAL AND TELEGRAPH OFFICE, New Church Road, c. 1918.

THE NEW POST OFFICE AND CAFE, c. 1929. This was built on to the end of the old post office (above), on the corner of New Church Road and Old Church Road. It was run by postmaster Mr H. Coward who, amongst other things, published his own postcards of Uphill.

POST OFFICE TEA GARDENS. These were at the junction of Old Church Road and Ellesmere Road, opposite the post office. Westfield House can be seen on the left.

ANOTHER VIEW of the Post Office Tea Gardens, c. 1920. The sign to the left reads 'Jay Bros. Mineral Waters', a Weston-super-Mare firm. The man in the doorway is pouring a glass of ginger beer from a stoneware bottle.

OLD CHURCH ROAD. A peaceful scene in the 1930s.

UPHILL FARM. This house was built in around 1620 and is the oldest domestic building in the village. It was once home to the lord of the manor.

MANOR FARM, looking west towards the old church.

LINKS ROAD, c. 1930. Berkeley Crescent is being built on the left. The sign is advertising the 'Links Guest House with Tea Garden and Lounge'.

LINKS ROAD after the devastating gales and floods of 13 December 1981. A new sea wall has now been built to try to prevent a repeat occurrence.

BEACH ROAD (now Links Road), c. 1910. The area on the left was part of Uphill Brickworks.

Uphill Church & Rocks.

UPHILL OLD CHURCH AND QUARRY, c. 1910. Brickyard Cottages can just be seen on the left.

OLD CHURCH ROAD, c. 1922.

THE OLD CHURCH OF ST NICHOLAS. The sign on the end wall of the Dolphin Inn is advertising Ross & Company's mineral waters, which were made in Weston-super-Mare.

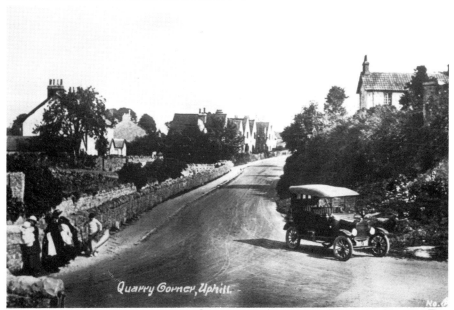

QUARRY CORNER, c. 1928. Steep Holm Cottages can be seen in the centre distance. The family seem all set for a day on the beach. The boy is carrying a deckchair.

A VIEW LOOKING DOWN OLD CHURCH ROAD, from the hill, with the light corrugated iron roof of Victory Hall in the centre left. This was built in 1952.

OLD CHURCH ROAD. St Nicholas' church tower is in the distance. Building started on a new church in 1841 due to the dilapidated state and inconvenient position of the old church. It was consecrated three years later.

ANOTHER VIEW OF OLD CHURCH ROAD, c. 1918. Uphill School can be seen in the centre here.

MRS THORN outside the Tuck Shop in the 1930s. This is now part of Walnut Cottage in Old Church Road.

BILL MINIFIE at the Forge, Sandcroft Cottages, Uphill Road.

AN OPEN-AIR SERVICE at St Nicholas Old Church, c. 1910. Regular services here were discontinued on 5 April 1846. Once a year, though, Holy Communion was celebrated 'in commemoration of the dead'.

UPHILL OLD CHURCH AND QUARRY, c. 1920.

THE INTERIOR of Uphill Old Church, photographed by R.W. Brown of Weston-super-Mare.

THE CARDIFF PILOT CUTTER *RUTH* at Uphill Pill. Vessels, such as colliers, of up to 120 tons, used Uphill Wharf.

UPHILL OLD CHURCH AND BREAN DOWN, *c.* 1930. This view was taken from the old windmill.

SECTION EIGHT

Brean Down

BREAN DOWN FERRY from Uphill, c. 1920. The building in the distance is Brean Down Farm.

BREAN DOWN FORT, C. 1923. The barracks were built in 1867 to provide accommodation for 51 men and 20 horses of the Coast Brigade, Royal Artillery, in case of attack from the French. The building was designed with a flat roof so any slates, displaced by firing, would not fall on the men. The smudges on the horizon are a warship and a small paddlesteamer.

The Old Fort, Brean Down, The Moat.

THE MOAT at Brean Down Fort.

BREAN DOWN FORT. In the 1920s the building became a tea-garden and restaurant. The entrance was by this bridge over the moat.

THE OLD FORT. When the fort was a tea-garden, this area was a playground for children, with swings and see-saws. On the left is one of the ammunition magazines.

THE THATCHED COTTAGE photographed by Charlie Pearson of Burnham-on-Sea, c. 1910.

COASTGUARD, HARRY COX, keeps watch over Brean Sands in 1943. Note the anti-aircraft and anti-landing craft defences on the beach.

BREAN DOWN FARMHOUSE RESTAURANT, c. 1920.

THE FARM, c. 1910.

PART OF THE MAKESHIFT PLAYGROUND at Brean Down Fort Restaurant, c. 1925.

A VIEW OF BREAN DOWN FORT from the beach. Note the clear limestone rock strata. This beach is rapidly covered by an incoming tide and many holidaymakers have been stranded here, often needing the lifeboat to rescue them.

SECTION NINE

Bleadon

BLEADON VILLAGE AND CHURCH, C. 1910.

BLEADON CHURCH AND POST OFFICE, c. 1910. The old village cross is to the left of the church. This view is much the same today.

BLEADON VILLAGE AND POST OFFICE, c. 1910. The top of the old village cross can be seen to the right of the man on the horse.

BLEADON CHURCH, C. 1910. This church is dedicated to St Peter and St Paul and is probably of Saxon foundation. However, most of the present church is of the Perpendicular period.

BLEADON RECTORY, C. 1908.

MULBERRY FARM GUEST HOUSE, c. 1920. This farm took its name from a 300-year-old mulberry tree in the garden. This was one of many hundreds of such trees planted in England during the reign of King James I, who encouraged the development of an English sericulture.

GODDEN'S TEA GARDENS, c. 1908.

BLEADON VILLAGE, c. 1910. The first of the carts is laden with large milk churns.

THE SQUARE, c. 1910. The road to Loxton is on the right with Bleadon Hill ahead.

THIS WOODEN BUNGALOW was situated nearly opposite Bleadon & Uphill Station.

ROCKVILLE HOUSE and the quarry, c. 1908. The shop belonged to G. Hawtin.

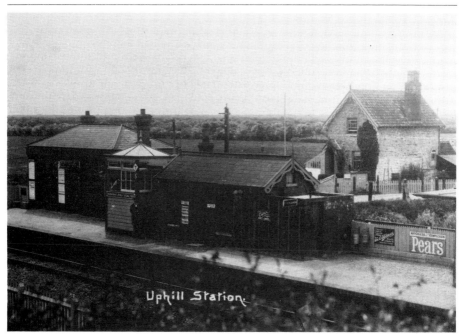

BLEADON & UPHILL STATION. This pretty Great Western Railway station has long been closed, although the buildings remain. For many years it housed a private railway museum.

BLEADON & UPHILL STATION AGAIN. This time a southbound mixed goods and passenger train is passing through. Enamel signs advertise Van Houtens' Cocoa.

THE GIPSY ENCAMPMENT at the quarry near Uphill & Bleadon Station.

MEMBERS OF THE JOULES FAMILY of gipsies in their camp at Bleadon quarry.

THESE VILLAGERS are believed to be members of the Joules gipsy family. The photograph was taken on 12 August 1892 by Charles Grinfield of Weston-super-Mare.

WONDERSTONE, C. 1911. This is on the road to Loxton, just out of Bleadon village.

PURN, near Bleadon, C. 1907. The pub on the left is The Anchor. A traction engine or road roller can just be seen disappearing around the corner. The wagon is laden with timber. The large enamel advertising sign reads 'Dunlop Tyre Stock S.R. Feaver, 87 High Street, Weston-super-Mare.'

BLEADON FROM THE QUARRY, C. 1920. In this view Bleadon Hill has not yet been developed.

A GENERAL VIEW OF BLEADON from the quarry, C. 1949. This picture has been taken from a similar viewpoint to the one above, but here houses have been built on Bleadon Hill.

THE TOLL-GATE, c. 1900. Owned by the General Estates Company at this time, the firm charged a toll for the use of the section of privately owned road between Bleadon & Uphill Station and Uphill. In the last year of its use it raised £500. It was originally erected to compensate the owner for having built the road.

THE REMOVAL OF BLEADON TOLL-GATE. At noon on 1 October 1908, the gate was ceremonially unhinged and removed. The owners were paid £3,000 and the road became the property of Weston Council. After the ceremony a luncheon was attended at Glass' Restaurant, Weston-super-Mare.

TWO PHOTOGRAPHS showing the building of the cutting between Uphill and Bleadon on the new A370 road in 1932. W.J. King of Bishops Lydeard were the contractors.

ACKNOWLEDGEMENTS

My thanks must go in the first instance to Woodspring Museum and its curator at the time, Jane Evans, for permission to draw freely upon their photographic collection. I am also indebted to Mrs Fry, who generously allowed me the use of her extensive postcard collection of the area.

Many other people and local societies have kindly supplied me with pictures and information, these being;

Mr Ballam • Banwell Society of Archaeology • Mr Cook • Mr Coward
Mrs J. Dunston • Mrs Edwards • Mr Farler • Mr and Miss Gunning
Mrs Harper • Mr J. Hunt • Linda Jenkins • Mrs McArdle • Miss Raines
Mrs Ryall • Betty Tabrett • Mr and Mrs Taylor • Mr P. Walters.

I would also like to thank Michael Tozer for his assistance.

I have made every endeavour to ensure that the captions in this book are correct. If you have any further information it will be gratefully received and can be forwarded by means of the publishers, Alan Sutton Publishing.

KEWSTOKE MEWS, Hatley, nr Kewstoke, c. 1914. Mr Weakley junior owned this wheelwright and carpenter's workshop in Kewstoke Road.